How co
God of
send people
to
HELL?

JOHN BENTON

EVANGELICAL PRESS

EVANGELICAL PRESS
Faverdale North, Darlington DL3 0PH, England

First published 1985
Second impression 1995
Third impression 2003

British Library Cataloguing in Publication Data
Benton, John, *1949-*
How can a God of love send people to hell?
1. Hell
I Title
236′.25 BT836.2

ISBN 0-85234-216-0

Bible quotations in this publication are from tne New International Version, Hodder & Stoughton, 1979

Printed in Great Britain by Cox and Wyman Ltd, Reading.

No one loses you, except one who voluntarily
leaves you. And if he leaves you, where can he go,
or where can he escape from you? He can only
run from your kindness to your anger. Everywhere
in his own punishment he will encounter your law.
And your law is truth, and truth is you.

Augustine of Hippo

Contents

1.
A controversial subject

In every single letter of the apostle Paul (except the short personal letter to Philemon), there is some reference to God's wrath. He speaks frequently of judgement, of destruction, of future condemnation. As a modern person, you may find this shocking and staggering.

However, it is true to say that Jesus has more to say on the subject of future punishment than anyone else in the New Testament. Concerning many topics Christ simply sows a few seed thoughts and leaves it to others, his apostles, to explain the subject fully. But it seems that with this matter of future punishment, knowing what a serious and controversial subject it is, he took upon himself the responsibility of speaking most plainly and most often about it. It is from the lips of Jesus that we hear of the fire that is never quenched and the worm which never dies (Mark 9:48; Matthew 10:28). It is Jesus who tells us of those suffering in outer darkness (Matthew 22:13).

The doctrine of future punishment is in the very warp and weft of the Christian message. It is an inescapable part of the fabric of the New Testament. When Christians speak about being 'saved', it is rescue from this eternal judgement which is uppermost in their minds. That eternal punishment for our sins is what we are saved from in particular. This is why there is such a stress in the New Testament on the urgent need for people to have their sins forgiven through faith in the Lord Jesus Christ. This is what brought Jesus on his mission of rescue, which led him to death on the cross. The Christian is the one whom Paul describes as having 'turned to God . . . to serve the living and true God; and to wait for his Son from heaven, whom he raised from the dead – Jesus, who rescues us from the coming wrath' (1 Thessalonians 1:9, 10).

So it is that once you have come to a grasp of what Christianity is saying, you may well have a question. Understanding the drift of the New Testament's message you ask, 'How can a God of love possibly send people to hell?'

'How can he?' This is a most serious question and one which is very frequently asked. Usually it is a very honest question. People find it genuinely difficult to reconcile the idea of God's love with that of eternal punishment.

Not surprisingly, emotions can run high. Confronted with the teaching concerning judgement, some people angrily reject the God of the Bible. He is accused of being callous, belligerent and primitive. The final irony occurs when the Bible itself is condemned as 'unchristian' because of its teaching on God's wrath. But strength of feeling on this subject is understandable. Heaven and hell are the most serious and solemn matters we can ever contemplate and to raise such serious matters may cause people to question at the deepest possible level the way that they are living their lives.

Faced with accusations of God seeming to be callous and monstrous in his judgement, the church has often panicked and backed away. Its response has frequently been to defect from the biblical teaching and to mutilate the character of God as revealed in Scripture, making him nothing but love and sweeping under the carpet the fact that there are more explicit references in the Bible to God's wrath than to his love.[1] Others within the church have responded by trying to reinterpret the Bible's teaching on hell in some way, reducing it merely to a graphic description of the psychological agony of the experience of guilt, or teaching purgatory or the annihilation of sinners rather than their perpetual punishment.

But do these theories really do justice to the serious statements of Jesus on the subject of God's wrath? He never seems to mention purgatory or annihilation. In his story of the rich man and Lazarus Jesus sets before us a most vivid picture of hell: 'The rich man also died and was buried. In hell, where he was in torment, he looked up and saw Abraham [in heaven] far away, with Lazarus by his side. So he called to him, "Father Abraham, have pity on me and send Lazarus to dip the tip of his finger in water and cool my tongue, because I am in agony in this fire." But Abraham replied, "Son, remember that in your lifetime you received your good things, while Lazarus received bad things, but now he is comforted here and you are in agony. And besides all this, between us and you a great chasm has been fixed, so that those who want to go from here to you cannot, nor can anyone cross over from there to us" ' (Luke 16:22–26).

'How can a God of love send people to hell?' is a question which people can use hotly to protest their opposition and rejection of Christianity. It is also a question through which people in a calmer mood can express sincere doubts and uncertainty about the validity of the Christian faith.

Working on the assumption that the New Testament documents give a reliable account of the authentic teaching of Christ and his apostles, this book seeks to sketch that teaching which concerns hell, to argue for its integrity and to set out the message of Christ in the light of it.

2.
Why is God angry?

The issues raised by the question we are considering may be so painful to you that you despise God and want to have nothing to do with him. But before we reject anything, it is as well to understand properly what we are rejecting, lest we make the mistake of judging by superficial appearances, having misunderstood the actual situation. So, before turning away, let us ask what is the context in which the Bible speaks of people going to hell? What is the Bible actually saying?

We must begin by realizing what the biblical view is of the present state of mankind. It is strikingly different from most current ideas.

1. Made in God's image

Neither Jesus nor the Bible as a whole sees the origin of our world or of human beings as an accident of nature. This world is the creation of God. He is its Maker. He is its Owner. In particular the Bible teaches the immense dignity of every single human being. We each carry the image of

God. We are like no other creatures, in that something of the character of the infinite person who is God is reflected in each one of us. This means that each and every man, woman and child is precious to God. He loves us all. It also explains why even people who reject God and deny his existence are often such nice people. Whether we acknowledge God or not, something of his image is still stamped upon us all.

2. God's plan for living

Because God has given us our existence and because every good and wholesome thing we have ever enjoyed has come to us from his hands, we are responsible to him for the way we live our lives. Our modern world sees morality as a very personal matter. It is for each individual to decide how to live his or her life. It is for everyone to be true to themselves. And indeed many people conscientiously do their best to abide by the standards they have set themselves. They do try to live by their own personal ethical code. But, with respect, the Bible would say this is to miss the point. It is not for us to set our own standards of behaviour, but for God to set them. This is his world. We are his creatures. God has rights over us.

More than that, God is not being authoritarian in a heavy-handed way when he wants to tell mankind how to live. He has in fact a responsibility to tell us what is right; otherwise we finite people, left in ignorance, not knowing how to live, might wander unknowingly into danger. Just as a father feels responsible to guide his children so that they do not run into danger and harm themselves, so God felt responsible to tell us how to live in the world he had made.

A brief summary of our Maker's instructions to us is contained, for example, in the Ten Commandments found in the Bible in Exodus 20 and Deuteronomy 5. These can be paraphrased as follows:

As God's creatures we have obligations towards him.
1. He is to be our God, the one we worship and no other.
2. We should worship him in the way he requires and deserves and not misrepresent him in any way.
3. We should not use God's name thoughtlessly or as a swear word.

Because we are made in the image of God, if we fail to acknowledge him, there is a sense in which we devalue ourselves. It might well be argued that the increasing secularization of our world is bringing with it a distinct diminishing of the worth of the individual and of human rights in the eyes of the law.

God has told us that we need a balanced cycle of work and rest and that true rest (of heart and soul) is only found through coming to him. God's day of rest is a good gift to us.
4. We should work during the week, but should keep Sunday as a day of rest which we specially set aside to meet with God.

God has made the family as the basic unit of society. In our parents we have something of a picture of God. They are our 'creators'. In their love for us we have a picture of the love of God for us. So God commands us that

5. We should love and respect our parents and obey them.

God has made us to relate to other people in the world and his basic rules for this aspect of our lives are:

6. We must not hate or murder other people, but rather love them.
7. We must not commit adultery, either physically or in our thoughts.
8. We must not steal from anyone.
9. We must not tell lies.
10. We must not be envious of what other people possess.

In other words, we are to love God and to love our fellow human beings made in his image. These laws give a good and practical framework for life, in which the rights and dignity of the individual are respected and love to our fellow men is encouraged. One writer in the New Testament describes them as 'the perfect law that gives freedom' (James 1:25).

Man has rejected God

In its opening chapters, having told us about God the Creator, the Bible goes on to speak of man's rejection of God. Man the creature, who owed everything to God, arrogantly turned his back on God. We sometimes speak of people 'biting the hand that feeds them', referring to the foolishness and perverse wickedness of their action. This is precisely what man has done. Man desired to be autonomous, to be answerable to no one, so he rebelled against God's authority over him, rejecting his loving Maker's instructions. This is the essence of what the Bible calls sin.

The effects of sin upon the world have been disastrous. God's beautiful creation was spoiled and the hearts of all men and women have become selfish, egotistical and petty. As mankind rejected God, the hatred, immorality, greed, suffering and confusion which have dominated history entered man's world.

How vehement is man's rejection of God? Is it mild opposition or is it spiteful hatred? How bad is the rift between God and man? It is always difficult to estimate oneself in any area of life. We rarely find it easy to have a balanced view where we are personally involved. But it is particularly difficult to estimate ourselves in this matter of our attitude towards God. We are so very far from unbiased. We automatically tend to justify ourselves. But we do have one clear indication of how vehement the human rejection of God has been. When God came and lived among us in his Son, Jesus Christ, how did we treat him? We *crucified* him.

Superficially looking at all the religion that is practised in the world, it would seem that man wants God. But when actually confronted with him in Jesus, it was the religious people who had him killed. Man wants God, but only a tame god, a 'god' who conforms to our desires, a 'god' who is man-made. He does not want the God who is actually there. Although it is almost universally acknowledged that the life of Jesus was blameless and that his ethical teaching is the most exalted known among mankind, yet there is something so wrong with the human heart that Jesus ended up on a cross. Speaking about himself, Jesus put it like this: 'This is the verdict: Light has come into the world, but men loved darkness instead of light because their deeds were evil. Everyone who does evil hates the light, and will not come into the light for fear that his deeds will be exposed' (John 3:19, 20).

The judgement of God

So, when we ask the question, 'How can a God of love send people to hell?' we are not asking quite the right question. When we frame the question in those words there is a subtle distortion of what the Bible is saying. The word 'people' is a neutral word and it gives the impression that, starting with a purely neutral situation, God is prepared capriciously to expose human beings to the excruciating agony of hell. But that is a terrible perversion of what Christianity is saying.

God's wrath is poured out, not because God is a nasty God, a sadistic God, who simply likes seeing his creatures suffer. God is not like a schoolboy who may set up his toy soldiers on the battlefield of the dining room table only to sweep them all flat, just to see the effect. The judgement of God is not expressed irrationally or against man simply because man is a weak creature and God wants to show his power. God is not like that and the Bible would regard it as the height of blasphemy to suggest that he was.

No, God's wrath has a particular stimulus. It is aroused by human sin. If there was no sin, there would be no wrath. It is aroused because of the human pursuit of that which is inherently bad – the selfishness, the lies, the arrogance.

Man's sin

The apostle Paul puts it like this: 'The wrath of God is being revealed from heaven against all the godlessness and wickedness of men' (Romans 1:18). He then goes on to list some of the sins which comprised the godlessness and wickedness of his own day in the first-century Roman world: 'Even their women exchanged natural relations for unnatural ones. In the same way the men also abandoned natural relations with women and were inflamed with lust for one another. Men committed indecent acts with other men, and received in themselves the due penalty for their perversion. Furthermore, since they did not think it worthwhile to retain the knowledge of God, he gave them over to a depraved mind, to do what ought not to be done. They have become filled with every kind of wickedness, evil, greed and depravity. They are full of envy, murder, strife, deceit and malice. They are gossips, slanderers, God-haters, insolent, arrogant and boastful; they invent ways of doing evil; they disobey their parents; they are senseless, faithless, heartless, ruthless' (Romans 1:26–31). An honest appraisal of our own society shows that things have not changed with mankind. We may like to view them in a different way; we may not call them 'sin' any longer. But the truth is that people are still involved in exactly the same things. Between the first and the twentieth centuries little has changed except the scenery. The things which make the news headlines are the same. And Paul would warn us that what was sin then is sin now, no matter what label we stick on it, and it will expose *us* to the coming wrath of God.

There are still many good things in people; we are made in God's image. But the good does not make up for the bad. We ought to be good all the time. Good may be there, but sin is also very much a part of our lives. We often only want to see the good, but reality forces us to admit the bad also.

It is not only Christians who recognize the sinful in man. Thoughtful people of many persuasions have drawn attention to human corruption throughout the ages. Writing one of the seminal books on politics, the fifteenth-century Italian Niccolo Machiavelli had to decide what were the characteristics of man's nature. He decided that man's nature, while actually good and bad, had to be treated, for the purposes of politics, as bad. Thus his book *The Prince* is littered with such statements as that 'Men are wicked and will not keep faith with you,' and that 'Unless men are compelled to be good they will inevitably turn out bad.'[2] Machiavelli may be accused of many things, but no one has ever accused him of not being a realist. Coming down to modern times, the great playwright George Bernard Shaw surveyed the history of mankind and concluded, 'The life of the human race is a brief discreditable episode in the history of the meanest of planets.'[3]

Such quotations could easily be multiplied. Sin is in man and it is sin which arouses God's wrath. If we are not to misunderstand and misrepresent what the Bible is teaching, we must not use neutral terms. God does not send *people* to hell; he sends *sinners* to hell. Sin is mankind's greatest problem. Sin is my greatest problem and yours.

'How can a God of love send *sinners* to hell?' That is the question and the nub of that question can now be explored in the following chapters.

3.
Current ideas about punishment

'Isn't God horrible? Isn't he vindictive and harsh to punish people for their sins?' Often that is how people react when Christians speak to them of sin and judgement.

Twentieth-century Western society has become deeply suspicious of the whole concept of punishment for wrongdoing. Our judicial and prison systems tend to want to deal with criminals purely in terms of deterring them or reforming them, not in terms of punishing them. Please do not get me wrong – the Bible is all for would-be criminals being deterred and bad characters being reformed. In many ways that is what the whole good news of the Lord Jesus Christ is about. People can be changed radically through the power of Christ. But we have lost sight of the idea of just punishment as a concept. The European courts have recently outlawed corporal punishment in schools. Down the last thirty years innumerable modern psychologists, from Dr Spock to the magazine agony aunts, have told us that the whole idea of punishment is bad.

Living in what has been termed a post-Christian era, when the influence of the Bible has drastically declined, our society has taken what it has estimated as best in Christian ethics and rejected the rest. We see ourselves as a caring society, a tolerant society – and, indeed, these things are not without their virtues. We see ourselves as a humanitarian society, an understanding society, in which the concept of punishment has no place.

Why is our culture so suspicious of punishment? Why do people reject the idea of just punishment and especially of God punishing anybody? I want to suggest that it has to do with certain outlooks and assumptions which make up the ethos of our century and form the background for our lives and thinking. We will consider some of them as we reflect on the Bible's teaching on judgement.

The greatest good?

How are we to live our lives and construct our morality? In a society which has come to live without reference to God, this is quite a problem. Who is to decide what is right and what is wrong? The answer to this question which seems to influence most the thinking of Western people is the idea that human happiness is the highest good. Broadly speaking, whatever brings the greatest good to the greatest number of people determines what is right.

Historically this outlook is known as 'utilitarianism'. It is an outlook which has much affinity with the concept of democracy which we all value in the Western world. One should pursue the principle of the greatest good, or the greatest happiness for the greatest number. That is the way we often see things and, of course, it easily leads to the finger of accusation being pointed at God when the subject of judgement is mentioned. God should not think of punishing us; he should only think about doing us good.

Now let us say immediately that bringing happiness and joy to people is a tremendous thing and God does love mankind and desires to see us happy. As we shall see, he desires that with a passion greater than we will ever understand. But this suspiciously self-centred principle of 'happiness for us' unfortunately will not serve as a definition of what is right.

This was made very obvious to me, for example, in an old cinema film. The story of the film was set in the southern states of the USA a few years ago. Someone has been murdered and the racially prejudiced townspeople are absolutely convinced that a black fellow is the murderer. But he isn't. The sheriff is faced with a terrible dilemma. Unless he hangs the man there will be terrific violence and rioting, with the probability of many people being killed. But the man is honestly innocent. What is he to do? The utilitarian principle of the greatest good for the greatest number would tend in the direction of hanging the man to save lives. But he is innocent.

You see, the greatest happiness for the greatest number is a fine priority, but it can never serve as a basis for justice. It cannot give us a proper definition of right and wrong. Now what is interesting in the situation depicted in the film is this. If the man had been hanged, we know and feel deeply within us that although it might have saved lives and pacified people, it would have been terribly unjust. Utilitarianism cannot account for our natural intuitions about justice.

Why do we have these natural feelings about what is right and what is wrong? The Bible's answer is that it is because there are such things as truth, right and wrong and justice, which exist outside us and what we want. They are absolute. They are a reflection of the unchanging character of God, who made the world. When God created man in his own image he, as it were, wrote his moral standards, the commandments, on our hearts and consciences. Our feelings for justice, although they may have been eroded and damaged somewhat by sin, still indicate God's commands to us. Our consciences witness to the fact that you and I are creatures of God and we are answerable ultimately, not just to other human beings, but to him.

Determinism

The second idea which causes our society to be so suspicious of the concept of punishment is the idea that people are not really responsible for their actions. Our actions, our decisions are predetermined by other factors over which we have no control. Therefore we are not to blame. We are not responsible for our sins and therefore it is grossly unfair of God to punish people for their wrongdoings. We cannot be held responsible. We are not really guilty.

This idea is subtly comforting for us and has come to command great influence over the twentieth century. Its roots are found in many areas of thought, but notably in psychiatry, biology and sociology.

Let us consider the first two of that list of three. On one hand there are the Freudian psychiatrists who tell us that our personalities are formed at an early age in response to environmental and particularly parental influences. In later life, it is maintained, our tendencies to act and think in certain ways are to a very large extent determined by these early factors. Thus we cannot be blamed for our current attitudes and behaviour, since they follow inevitably from events and situations in the distant past as the result of a causal process over which we have had little or no control. So it is not our fault that we are the way we are and do what we do.

On the other hand, there are those of a more biological way of thinking who adhere to what we might term the medico-biological approach. Rejecting Freudianism as being far too speculative in its assumptions about the influence of our past on us, these people adopt what they consider to be a more scientific approach. They maintain that our behaviour and the kind of people we are are determined not so much by our past experiences as by the genetic information passed on to us by our parents and other ancestors. Our actions and attitudes are determined solely by our brain biochemistry. So, once again, it comes down to factors beyond our control governing us. Hence it is proposed, inevitably, that individuals cannot be blamed for their sins.

It can be seen, therefore, that both the Freudians and those who adopt the medico-biological approach and, indeed, anyone who might go in for a mixture of the two theories reach the same practical conclusion. The sinner is to be treated as a 'patient' rather than a responsible offender and sinful behaviour is fundamentally an 'illness' rather than a culpable act. We are not responsible. To punish a person because he is ill would be monstrously inappropriate and we have often carried that thinking over into the area of how we respond to all wrongdoing. In the words of C. S. Lewis, 'Thus it appears at first sight that we have passed from the harsh self-righteous notion of giving the wicked their deserts to the charitable and enlightened one of tending the psychologically sick.'[4]

The third root of the current idea of non-responsibility is a little different. It comes not first of all from biology or psychology, but from sociology. It does not look back particularly to the past, as the other two roots do, but looks primarily at the present. Our behaviour is the result of the environment in which we live. People commit crimes, commit sins of various kinds, because they come from deprived backgrounds, because their parents are divorced, because of their present housing conditions or conditions at work, etc.

Personally, I have a lot of sympathy with the general spirit of this idea. But nevertheless it needs to be considered honestly.

The non-responsibility implied in these three roots of thought is, whether consciously or unconsciously, tailor-made to comfort us sinners, because it neatly shifts the blame from our shoulders and puts it down elsewhere. Society is to blame. Our parents are to blame. The 'defects' in our genetic code are to blame. It is not our fault. How dare God hold us responsible for our sins!

However, having said all that and recognizing the vast influence of these ideas in the popular mind, such thinking is very inadequate and misleading.

No proof

Firstly, it is misleading because in all three areas we have considered, non-responsibility is not a carefully established conclusion, but rather an unquestioned, tacit assumption. Non-responsibility is uncritically built into all three of these roots. All three approaches seek to describe man 'scientifically'. But to decide to describe man scientifically is to presuppose a cause-effect relationship to govern man's behaviour. Cause-effect relationships are what science is all about. But it is left totally unproved as to whether or not human behaviour can be described so simplistically.

The facts don't fit

Secondly, when we do look at the 'experimental data' of human behaviour the assumption is rather embarrassed by the facts. To hold to such a strict deterministic outlook is simply to fly in the face of the facts of the real world.

It would be very foolish not to acknowledge

that all the things we have mentioned do have some influence upon our lives. But to clear us of all responsibility for our sins these factors have got to be proved, not just to be influential factors, but to be determining factors. It must be proved that they shut us in completely, so that there is no other option than to do as we have done. It must be proved that we are nothing but puppets to our genes, our upbringing and/or our environment. But that, quite simply, is not the case when we look at the facts.

For example, the following quotation comes from a major review of practice in dealing with juvenile offenders, which appeared in the journal *Social Work Today* in 1982. Considering the view of the offender as a mere victim of circumstance, the writer had to conclude, 'Although it may be generally valid that social, economic and personal disadvantage correlate highly with officially recorded juvenile offending behaviour, *there is no evidence that this is an adequate causal explanation*.' The writer also says, 'The most obvious area of criminal behaviour which counters the assumed causal relationship between disadvantage and crime is that of "white collar crime". Crimes of fraud and embezzlement are committed by individuals who have the opportunity available to them and by having it available are almost by definition not deprived.'[5]

Not everyone from a broken home and a poor background *has* to turn to a life of crime and the majority do not. Environment, although an influential factor, is simply not a determining factor. Our environment may increase our temptation to sin, but it does not make sin inevitable.

When we look at the biological and psychological theories of determinism we find precisely the same objection. In a recent controversial book even a non-Christian doctor takes the modern biological and psychological theories to task. Although they hold so much sway in our society, he accuses them of lacking evidence. He pleads for a return to the commonsense approach of generations past of holding people responsible for their own actions and highlights the dehumanizing effect which deterministic ideas have upon people. 'It may seem odd that the accumulated wisdom of generations could be pushed aside so easily when no irrefutable concrete evidence has been produced to discredit it. Certainly there is no conclusive proof that the metapsychological posturings of the psychodynamists have any relevance to the understanding of how we live our lives or have contributed towards increasing their quality. Similarly the biochemists have produced no substances that add in any worthwhile way to the psychological well-being of those who are not suffering from actual psychiatric illness.'[6]

Obviously there are in our society some people who are genuinely mentally ill and such people deserve the most loving understanding and attention. But to label all wrongdoers as sick, non-responsible people, just because they are wrongdoers is a terrible fallacy. It overlooks and covers up the downright perversity of the human heart, which we all know is there. There may be different pressures on different people, but these are not determining factors. A personal choice, for which we are responsible, is involved in our actions.

This is the position taken by the Bible. It recognizes that circumstances of one kind or another do influence people, but nevertheless in the final analysis it insists that we are responsible for our actions. There are mitigating circumstances, but not exonerating circumstances. Thus we find one of the writers of the book of Proverbs declaring, 'Give me neither poverty nor riches, but give me only my daily bread. Otherwise, I may have too much and disown you and say, "Who is the Lord?" Or I may become poor and steal, and so dishonour the name of my God' (Proverbs 30:8, 9). Circumstances can provide temptations, but circumstances do not control us. *We* choose. The rich man's wealth may tempt him to arrogance; the poor man's want may tempt him to steal, but their circumstances do not remove all responsibility from them.

Some words from the philosopher C. E. M. Joad are appropriate at this point. He was drawn towards Christian beliefs after many years of agnosticism and one of the things which brought him to this position was that he felt that deterministic ideas concerning human nature were tragically inadequate. The Christian explanation was far more convincing. In 1952 he wrote, 'What I have to record is a changed view of the nature of man, which in due course led to a changed view of the nature of the world . . . This view of human evil [that evil is merely the product of heredity and environment and can be eradicated through progress] which I adopted unthinkingly as a young man, I have come fundamentally to disbelieve. Plausible, perhaps, during the first fourteen years of this century when . . . the state of mankind seemed to be improving – though even then the most cursory reading of human history should have been sufficient to dispose of it – it has been rendered utterly implausible by the events of the last forty years. To me, at any rate, the view of evil implied by Marxism, expressed by Shaw and maintained by modern psychotherapy, a view which regards evil as a by-product of circumstances, which circumstances can, therefore, alter and even eliminate, has come to seem intolerably shallow and the contrary view of it as endemic in man, more particularly in its Christian form, the doctrine of original sin, to express a deep and essential insight into human nature.'[7]

Jesus' explanation of sin is not the environment; it is the human heart. Sin comes not from what is outside us, but from what is inside us. He said, 'From within, out of men's hearts, come evil thoughts, sexual immorality, theft, murder, adultery, greed, malice, deceit, lewdness, envy, slander, arrogance and folly. All these evils come from inside and make a man unclean' in the sight of God (Mark 7:21–23).

The myth of remedial punishment

Thirdly, the idea that deterministic views of 'treatment' for offenders is more humane than justice and punishment has been shown, both in theory and practice, to be a myth. In the face of ideas which speak in terms of the reform of the criminal being the only worthwhile aim, our society has felt uneasy about the biblical concept of punishment and has often rejected it. We must, of course, as I have said before, long to see criminals reformed. But we should not be so hasty to lay the biblical teaching on one side.

We need to remember that if the 'cure' of criminals is to be the only aim, then it leads in a very sinister direction indeed. I will let C. S. Lewis explain. He was reading an article in which 'the author was pleading that a certain sin, now treated by our laws as a crime, should henceforward be treated as a disease. And he complained that under the present system the offender, after a term in gaol, was simply let out . . . where he would probably relapse. What he complained of was not the shutting up – but the letting out. On his remedial view of punishment, the offender should of course be detained until he was cured . . . the first result of the humanitarian theory is, therefore, to substitute for a definite sentence (reflecting to some extent the degree of the crime) an indefinite sentence,'[8] terminable only when experts believe the man cured. Thus the door is open for greater punishment than justice requires, which is hardly a kind or humane situation.

C. S. Lewis' theorizing has been found to be only too true in practice. In the article previously referred to, which considered the treatment of juvenile offenders, the writer states, 'The final criticism of the welfare approach is that indeterminacy of sentence to allow for individual progress in treatment actually leads to longer periods of incarceration than determinate sentencing under the justice model.' The writer had previously declared, 'When as a clinical psychologist I worked in a hospital for the mentally handicapped which had among its facilities a discharge hostel for patients from a special hospital, it soon became obvious to me that many of these patients had been held in special hospitals for extremely long periods, many in fact for periods far in excess of the prison sentence predictable from their offence.'[9]

The idea of just punishment is often caricatured as hard and unfeeling, but that need not be the case. The whole point of just punishment is that it is just. It sets a proper limit to society's retribution.

God's judgement is impeccably just. Anger in human beings is invariably accompanied by sin. But when we think of God's wrath we must not have any idea of unrestrained anger, or of God indulging in a thoughtless frenzy of punishment. God's judgement is carried out with the greatest and most precise justice and control. The Bible insists that he is 'a faithful God who does no wrong, upright and just is he' (Deuteronomy 32:3, 4). And God's judgement is not without mercy. He offers free mercy and forgiveness to us in the Lord Jesus Christ. It is only those who refuse Christ who are exposed to God's just punishment. Jesus said, 'Whoever believes in the Son has eternal life, but whoever rejects the Son will not see life, for God's wrath remains on him' (John 3:36).

Human error

The third major reason which has caused our twentieth-century world to be suspicious of the concept of just punishment is the possibility of human error in the courts. The police and the judiciary are capable of making mistakes. Recent cases in Britain have shown that people have been convicted and have served prison sentences on the mistaken evidence of forensic scientists. Perhaps one of the greatest arguments which persuade many people that it is right to maintain the abolition of capital punishment is the possibility of carrying out this ultimate sentence only to find later that a mistake has been made. Obviously we should take every possible precaution to safeguard the courts from error, but we still have to confess that such errors are real possibilities.

But this objection to just punishment has no place when we come to consider God's judgements. He is never misinformed. He alone is aware of every possible extenuating circumstance. The things which may be hidden from men are impossible to hide from God. The New Testament puts it like this: 'Nothing in all creation is hidden from God's sight. Everything is uncovered and laid bare before the eyes of him to whom we must give account' (Hebrews 4:13). Although the matter of error may be something to be considered in connection with human justice, it has no place in the matter of the judgement of the God of the Bible.

People may not agree with Christianity, but

the integrity of what it speaks of is very difficult to fault. As we have examined the kinds of reasons why modern people are suspicious of the concept of just punishment, the Bible and the facts of experience give solid answers as to why Christianity declares that people are responsible for their sins and that God will judge us unless we are saved.

The character of God

So far in this chapter we have looked at some reasons why modern people tend to be suspicious of the idea of just punishment which underlies the biblical teaching of future condemnation. We have looked especially at the ideas of utilitarianism and determinism. But some people have a more fundamental problem with the insistence of the Bible and of Christianity upon God's just punishment. They find it very difficult to believe that God is actually concerned about sin and especially about how we as individuals live our lives.

People say something like this: 'I can understand God being concerned about international political situations and the sins of multi-national companies against the Third World, but I can't believe that he is actually concerned about personal sin. Not respecting parents, ignoring Jesus, lying to the customer at work about when his order will be ready, coveting things that do not belong to me, I can't believe that God really cares about these things. Greed is so common. I can't believe that God will really respond with wrath and judgement on personal sin.'

I sometimes wonder if such a response has something to do with the way our perception of what is important is influenced by the way the news media report what goes on in the world. We may tend to think, 'The ordinary suburban adultery does not make the headlines of the national dailies or the TV news, so it can't be all that important.' But it is a moot point as to whether the priorities of the producers of news programmes coincide with those of God. However, leaving that aside, this objection basically comes down to a matter of the character of God. 'Is God actually that kind of God? Does he really care about sin? I can't believe it.'

But in answer to this it must be said that it is illogical to think that because you cannot believe something, it cannot be true. Surely the mistake in such thinking is clear. You cannot believe that God is like that, you cannot believe that he will do this or that and therefore you draw the conclusion that he is not like that or he will not do that. In other words, God can only do or be what you think. But, as in every other area of life, it is not what you think or you wish which counts, it is what is. And that can be and often is very different from what we think.

How many of us wish that such things as nuclear weapons had never been invented? How many of us feel that the world would be far better off if the possibility of such things had never been discovered? But that does not change the fact that nuclear weapons have been made and are stockpiled on both sides of the Atlantic.

All the way through the Bible we find that

we are warned that, although he is a God of love, a God who is slow to anger, yet nevertheless God is a God of judgement. This is a lesson from both the Old Testament and the New Testament.

In Old Testament times, God gave his written law to the nation of Israel and said that if they obeyed they would be blessed with prosperity and peace, but if they despised his instructions and rebelled against him, he would punish them and we find just this happening again and again in the biblical narrative. In the New Testament, God sends Christ to save us and through him the world is to be called back to God, but for all who reject Christ there is to be judgement. 'In the past God overlooked such ignorance, but now he commands all people everywhere to repent. For he has set a day when he will judge the world with justice' (Acts 17:30, 31).

We are to have every sympathy for what has happened to the Jewish people over the last 2000 years, for we are sinners too. But how does the Bible interpret it? God made them a nation and God gave them his law. They were privileged above all other people on earth. But then he warned them, 'If you do not carefully follow all the words of this law . . . then the Lord will scatter you among all nations, from one end of the earth to the other . . . Among those nations you will find no repose, no resting place for the sole of your foot. There the Lord will give you an anxious mind, eyes weary with longing and a despairing heart. You will live in constant suspense, filled with dread both night and day, never sure of your life. In the morning you will say, "If only it were evening!" and in the evening, "If only it were morning!" – because of the terror that will fill your hearts and the sights that your eyes will see' (Deuteronomy 28:58, 64–67). Having rebelliously rejected their Messiah Jesus, whom God sent to them, this is precisely what has happened to dear Jewish people. Scattered all over the globe and often persecuted, it is only since 1949 that some of the Jews have returned to the land God promised them. Sadly their history is an eloquent testimony which provides us with evidence, right down to this very day, that God is a God of judgement, who is concerned about personal sin.

But it would be wrong to single out the Jews alone. Jesus himself was not afraid to see evidence of the fact that the world is even now experiencing something of God's wrath in natural disasters and man's inhumanity to man. 'Now there were some present at that time who told Jesus about the Galileans whose blood Pilate had mixed with their sacrifices.' (Worshippers had been slaughtered.) 'Jesus answered, "Do you think that these Galileans were worse sinners than all the other Galileans because they suffered in this way? I tell you, no! But unless you repent, you too will all perish. Or those eighteen who died when the tower in Siloam fell on them – do you think they were more guilty than all the others living in Jerusalem? I tell you, no! But unless you repent, you too will all perish' (Luke 13:1–5).

Jesus is plain. God's wrath is already revealed against a sinful world and as individuals we need to repent. God is concerned about our sin, national and individual, corporate and personal.

4.
Jesus' teaching on hell

A universalist is a person who believes that, no matter what sins people may have committed and no matter how much people might reject God, ultimately it is impossible to escape God's love. Eventually, it is said, all people, every single individual who has ever lived, will be welcomed and accepted by God.

I am sure that there is a part in all of us which would like to believe that that was true. If not, we are in danger of becoming very hard and unloving people indeed. We sympathize with the emotions which draw some people in the direction of universalism. But, in all honesty, it is impossible to interpret Jesus as teaching universalism. As an idea it denies mankind the dignity and right of having our decisions in life, to accept God or reject him, taken seriously. Again, if everyone is saved, then Jesus' commission to his followers to preach the gospel and make disciples is pointless. People are going to be saved anyway. Universalism suffers from fatal defects. It is an alluring theory, but it does not fit the New Testament.

Christianity is founded on the teachings of

Christ and if we want to know what Christianity stands for, we must be prepared to face squarely what Jesus taught. In this chapter we will try to review what Jesus had to say concerning the subject of hell. What is the nature of the future punishment for sin of which he warned?

After life

Jesus clearly taught that this life is not the only existence. He spoke of life beyond death. He did this in many different ways. It was a tacit assumption behind much of his ethical teaching (Matthew 6:19, 20). He spoke often of 'the world to come', which all people would experience in one form or another (Matthew 12:32; Mark 10:30). He spoke of the great godly men of the Old Testament, who had died long before, continuing to live in the kingdom of heaven (Luke 13:28). He was ridiculed by the smart sceptics of his day for his belief in the resurrection of the dead at the end of the world (Mark 12:18–27). Of course, he spoke of his own continued existence after his death (John 10:18).

The outlook of philosophical materialism, which dominates the world-view current in the West in this century, often leads us to think that this life is all. We tend to construe life in terms of existence and death as non-existence. In fact, when the word 'death' is used in the Bible, it never means non-existence. Rather it is to be viewed in terms of separation. Physical death is seen, not as a full stop, but as the separation of a person's body and soul. The physical body may disintegrate by the natural processes of corruption, but the soul lives on. So the apostle Paul speaks of a Christian's death as a 'departure', not as a dead end (Philippians 1:23). For the Christian to die is to be 'away from the body and at home with the Lord' (2 Corinthians 5:8). Jesus spoke directly of two men dying and of their life beyond death, one in heaven and the other in hell (Luke 16: 19–31).

Again, the fact that death in the Bible denotes separation rather than oblivion is shown by the fact that Jesus can speak of people being 'dead' while they are physically alive. When someone comes to know God personally, Jesus speaks of that person as having 'crossed over from death to life' (John 5:24). The God of the Bible is the God who is the joyous fountain of bubbling vitality, light and life. The breath of his word called all creation into being (Genesis 1:3–27). At his touch the barren woman's womb is made fertile (Genesis 18:10–15). The desert blossoms with a delightful carpet of spring flowers as the Lord walks its paths (Isaiah 35:1, 2). These are just a few of the illustrations which the Bible uses to try to convey the vivifying and transforming life that flows from God. Life in the true meaning of the word is only to be had through being in touch with this marvellous Lord. Mere existence, life separate from God, is not life at all; it is a living death. So it is that when men and women turn to Christ and find God for themselves, Jesus speaks of them as passing from death to life. They have lived separate from God. They have been dead to

God. But now they have found the Lord and are in contact with him. They are alive.

For Jesus death means separation, not annihilation. Jesus never speaks of anyone ceasing to exist. Physical death is not the end. It is rather the tearing apart of soul and body. But the person, the soul, the real you, lives on.

Jesus also went on to teach that at the end of the world God will reconstruct people physically. All people will be raised from the dead, spirits rejoined to bodies, to face the final judgement as whole persons. All this might appear fantastic to the modern sceptic, yet the great miracle of Jesus' own resurrection foreshadows this profound event of the last day. 'Do not be amazed at this,' said Jesus, 'for a time is coming when all who are in their graves will hear his voice and come out – those who have done good will rise to live, and those who have done evil will rise to be condemned' (John 5:28, 29). Part of the reason why Jesus performed miracles of raising the dead was to underline what may seem incredible to us – that God has the power to raise the dead. To die is not to be beyond God. A teacher may write a word with his chalk on the blackboard and then rub it off. But that does not preclude him from writing that same word again. It should not surprise us that God is able to rewrite that bundle of genetic and psychological information which is us and draw us again on the blackboard of life, after we have died.

Jesus, then, taught continued existence after death. He taught the survival of the spiritual side of us after physical death. He taught the general resurrection at the end of the world.

When people's personal lives go wrong, when they get caught up in bitterness and anger, when perhaps there is vicious language and even violence in the family home, we sometimes speak of people creating 'hell on earth'. My own father survived the horrors of a Japanese prisoner-of-war camp. We think of the traumatic experiences in 1981 and 1985 of the people taken hostage on the hijacked American aircraft in Iran and Beruit. People speak of such terrible experiences as 'going through hell'. The psychological agony of guilt or the deep pain of bereavement are spoken of colloquially as being 'like hell'.

With such a usage of words it might seem very tempting to equate hell itself with some of the immense tragedies and physical and mental sufferings through which we may pass in life. But Jesus never speaks of hell in this way. As we have seen he taught a continued existence after death and he locates hell very definitely in the life to come. For example, Jesus said, 'I tell you, my friends, do not be afraid of those who kill the body and after that can do no more. But I will show you whom you should fear: Fear him who, after the killing of the body, has power to throw you into hell. Yes, I tell you, fear him' (Luke 12:4, 5). Hell comes after death. It is not part of this present life.

In Jesus' graphic story of the rich man and Lazarus the beggar, the same point is made with solemn poignancy. Jesus tells us, 'The time came when the beggar died and the angels carried him to Abraham's side. The rich man also died and was buried.' The very next words of Jesus, describing what had happened to the rich man, are these: 'In hell, where he was in torment, he looked up . . .' (Luke 16:22, 23).

For Jesus, hell is not part of this life, it is very much part of the world to come. When a person dies his or her spirit goes immediately either to the place of bliss and happiness or to the place of unspeakable torment. At the end of time, after the resurrection, those who in this life accepted God's offer of forgiveness will, with new bodies, be part of a transformed universe full of peace and joy. But those who have rejected God and continued in their sins will, according to Jesus, be thrown body and soul into hell.

So seriously does Jesus view these matters that he is prepared to use words such as the following to bring home to us the urgency of the situation: 'You have heard that it was said, "Do not commit adultery." But I tell you that anyone who looks at a woman lustfully has already committed adultery with her in his heart. If your right eye causes you to sin, gouge it out and throw it away. It is better for you to lose one part of your body than for your whole body to be thrown into hell. And if your right hand causes you to sin, cut it off and throw it away. It is better for you to lose one part of your body than for your whole body to go into hell' (Matthew 5:27–30). It was because Jesus knew the fearful consequences of sin and of rejecting God that he warned people with a loving bluntness and was prepared to go to the cross to rescue us.

What did he mean?

It is important to realize that the Bible is generally restrained in its language describing hell. It does not indulge in the vivid imaginative excesses of medieval artists. It does not use the lurid descriptions of Dante or Milton. But, as Herbert Carson has noted, 'It is significant that the most solemn utterances on this subject fall from the lips of Christ himself. In the New Testament as a whole there is a deep reserve on the nature of the punishment of the lost, though of course the act of final judgement is prominent. But with Christ himself the statements are much more explicit.'[10]

With such a weighty subject on our hands, this is no place to indulge in speculation and so the main aim of this chapter is simply to let the words of Jesus speak for themselves wherever possible, and to keep comments to a minimum.

What did Jesus teach about what happens after death to those who reject God? How did he describe what hell is? Underlying his teaching there seem to be three basic elements. Firstly, there is the misery caused by *what people are deprived of* in hell. The words Jesus uses to describe this deprivation are 'darkness' or 'the darkness outside'. Secondly, there is the misery caused by *what people are positively exposed to* in hell. Jesus speaks of this in terms of 'the fire of hell' or 'eternal fire'. Thirdly, Jesus speaks of hell as a place of *continual disintegration and dissolution.* He uses the figure of 'the worm that does not die'. It is a sobering and heart-rending categorization.

1. Deprivation

In this present life all people to some extent enjoy the blessings of God. We live in a world which is very far from perfect, yet there still remains in it much that is good. There is much tragedy in this world, but there is also joy. There is much hatred and selfishness in this world, but there is also love among family and friends. Sickness goes hand in hand with health. Dishonesty is mixed with truth. This world still knows many good things from God. But Jesus pictures hell as a state of being shut out from all God's goodness.

The figure of 'outer darkness' is referred to three times by Jesus in Matthew's Gospel.

Confronted with a Gentile, a Roman centurion, who showed great faith in him while all around there were Jews who rejected him, Jesus said, 'I say to you that many will come from the east and the west, and will take their places at the feast with Abraham, Isaac and Jacob in the kingdom of heaven. But the subjects of the kingdom will be thrown outside, into the darkness, where there will be weeping and gnashing of teeth' (Matthew 8:11, 12).

Jesus told a parable of a wedding banquet, to which everyone was invited to come and honour the king's son on his wedding day. The king in Jesus' parables often represents God and Jesus is his son. To honour the son at the wedding all the guests would attend in the finest wedding clothes appropriate to the occasion. But many whom the king invited would not attend and one man was found at the banquet who had not bothered to dress appropriately for the wedding.

He was 'only here for the beer', so to speak, not to honour the son. Jesus tells us that 'The king told the attendants, "Tie him hand and foot, and throw him outside, into the darkness, where there will be weeping and gnashing of teeth"' (Matthew 22:13).

Jesus told another parable of a wealthy man who had left his servants in charge of his money while he went away on a journey. He gave each servant a certain amount of cash and told them to do their best to invest it for him wisely. When the master returned he shared his fortune with those who worked for him. But one man was so indolent that he neglected to do anything for his master. When the master returned he was furious that the man had done nothing: 'Take the talent from him and give it to the one who has ten talents. For everyone who has will be given more, and he will have an abundance. Whoever does not have, even what he has will be taken from him. And throw that worthless servant outside, into the darkness, where there will be weeping and gnashing of teeth' (Matthew 25:28–30).

The context of all these sayings is that of a shared celebration, a feast of happiness. Imagine a great party held at night. Outside it is cold and bitter and dark. Inside the house the lights shine and through the window are seen the gaily decorated rooms and the bright lights and the sounds of joy are heard. Inside there is light, warmth, joy, festivity, celebration and delight. Outside is the opposite of all those things. Outside people look on at all the gaiety, wishing they were within, but they are shut out, deprived of all those things, cut off from it all. That is the picture which Jesus uses here. Hell is to be shut out from all joy, light and life. It is to be deprived of the good things you have tasted in life, but never appreciated. It is to be shut out of God's presence, cut off from all that is good and wholesome. It is to be cut off from all love, all peace, all joy for ever. Jesus explains that once people realize this, once they realize what they have missed, the effect upon them will be devastating: 'There will be weeping and gnashing of teeth.'

It is an unspeakably sombre picture. Men seldom weep, but in hell men weep uncontrollably. Jesus speaks of the place being totally characterized by tears. The Greek in which the New Testament was written includes the definite article in Jesus' words. It is not just 'weeping' in hell; it is '*the* weeping'. It is as if Jesus is saying that every connotation of what is involved when people shed tears on earth is summed up in the total distress of hell. All the tears of earth are just a preview to the sobs of hell. Here, in this life, men and women weep, but *the* weeping awaits.

Jesus also speaks of people 'gnashing their teeth' in hell. I used to wonder what that meant, but the Bible itself explains. A man called Stephen was the first Christian martyr. His story is recorded for us in the New Testament in chapters 6 and 7 of the book of Acts. He was a bold witness for Christ with a great intellectual gift. Stephen had brought such a powerfully convicting message to the Jerusalem authorities who were opposing Christianity and had so refuted all their arguments and proved his case that we read, 'When they heard this, they were furious and gnashed their teeth at him' (Acts 7:54). They went on to stone him to death. But, you see, the leading religious men in Jerusalem were so furious, so angry with Stephen that they could not speak – all they could do was gnash their teeth.

In hell people do not just weep; they gnash their teeth. Having been shut out of the presence of God into the eternal blackness, permanently deprived of all that is wholesome and good, in bitter anger men and women grind their teeth in speechless rage. As they realize that once and for all, 'I've been shut out!' they are overcome with a sense of eternal loss, which leads to a depth of anger and fury that they find impossible to express in words. What an awful picture is contained in the words of Jesus!

2. Punishment

But the miseries of hell do not just consist in the things of which men and women who have rejected God are deprived. Jesus speaks of positive punishment directed towards sinners. He speaks of this in terms of fire.

In the Sermon on the Mount Jesus gives warning about sins of the misuse of language and verbal abuse. He says, 'I tell you that anyone who is angry with his brother will be subject to judgement. Again, anyone who says to his brother, 'Raca' [an Aramaic term of contempt meaning something like 'numskull'], is answerable to the Sanhedrin. But anyone who says, 'You fool!' will be in danger of the fire of hell' (Matthew 5:22).

Jesus told a parable about a farmer who sowed good seed in his field, but later his enemy came and sowed weeds in among the good seed, making the field extremely difficult to harvest. Later Jesus explained the parable: 'The one who sowed the good seed is the Son of Man. The field is the world and the good seed stands for the sons of the kingdom. The weeds are the sons of the evil one, and the enemy who sows them is the devil. The harvest is the end of the age and the harvesters are angels. As the weeds are pulled up and burned in the fire, so it will be at the end of the age. The Son of Man will send out his angels, and they will weed out of his kingdom everything that causes sin and all who do evil. They will throw them into the fiery furnace, where there will be weeping and gnashing of teeth. Then the righteous will shine like the sun in the kingdom of their Father. He who has ears, let him hear' (Matthew 13:37–43).

Later in the same chapter of Matthew Jesus tells a similar parable to that of the good seed and the weeds – only this time it is about a fishing net which catches in it many different kinds of fish, good and bad. Eventually the good and bad are separated and again Jesus speaks of the bad being thrown into the fire (Matthew 13:47–50).

Another parable of separation is that of the sheep and the goats. It is such parables as these which make universalism, which we mentioned at the beginning of the chapter, untenable as reflecting the teaching of Jesus. Everyone does not end up in the same place. There is a separation.

In this parable the sheep are those who have loved and served the king; the goats are those who have ignored and never helped the king. The parable teaches us the terrible consequences of the sin of neglecting the poor and needy of the world. Jesus has the king saying these most terrible words to those he condemns: 'Depart from me, you who are cursed, into the eternal fire prepared for the devil and his angels. For I was hungry and you gave me nothing to eat, I was thirsty and you gave me nothing to drink, I was a stranger and you did not invite me in. I needed clothes and you did not clothe me, I was sick and in prison and you did not look after me . . . I tell you the truth, whatever you did not do for one of the least of these, you did not do for me' (Matthew 25:41–45). In speaking of hell Jesus uses the awesome picture of eternal fire.

To the south of Jerusalem in Bible times there was a valley called the valley of Hinnom, or in the Greek Gehenna. At one time it had been associated with the worship of a fearful idol called Molech, in connection with which child sacrifice was practised. But a major reform of the nation under the Old Testament king Josiah had led to the idol shrine being smashed down and the valley being made into the sewage pit of Jerusalem. Dead animals, the corpses of criminals and everything that was counted as rubbish were thrown into the valley and set on fire. The fire there burned continually and the valley became a symbol in the popular mind for the fire of hell.

Although the popular mind can often be wrong, Jesus endorsed this as an idea of what hell is like.

It is a place of ceaseless unquenchable fire. Jesus never tired of correcting the misconceptions of his day. One only has to recall that repeated refrain from the lips of Jesus in the Sermon on the Mount: 'You have heard that it was said . . . but I tell you . . . ,' to realize how outspoken he was against whatever was erroneous. Yet Jesus never tried to correct, but rather confirmed the idea of eternal fire. In this connection also Jesus speaks of the occupants of hell weeping and gnashing their teeth (Matthew 13:42, 50).

Jesus saw the consequences of sin as terrifying. He saw sin as leading people to this place of indescribable misery and so again he is shockingly urgent and direct in his warnings: 'Woe to the world because of the things that cause people to sin! Such things must come, but woe to the man through whom they come! If your hand or your foot causes you to sin, cut it off and throw it away. It is better for you to enter life maimed or crippled than to have two hands or two feet and be thrown into eternal fire. And if your eye causes you to sin, gouge it out and throw it away. It is better for you to enter life with one eye than to have two eyes and be thrown into the fire of hell' (Matthew 18:7–9). It is doubtful that Jesus meant us literally to mutilate ourselves, but he is using such strong language to drive home the fact that hell is such a horrendous destiny that we should spare no pains to avoid the sin that takes people there.

When people read the fearful descriptions of hell which come from Jesus, often they want to ask a question: 'Are these things to be taken literally? Are we to think of literal fire and literal darkness?'

As far as the precise nature of the darkness and fire of hell are concerned, it would be wise to avoid speculation. The fire 'prepared for the devil and his angels' (Matthew 25:41) must be something more than physical fire. We must grant that figurative language is being used and rest at that point. However, at the same time, we must reject the idea that because it is picture language, it holds no meaning and no fear for us. Let nobody think that it is only symbolical and therefore not so terrible. Rather we should realize that if the symbol, the mere picture, is already awe-inspiring, how horrible must the actual reality be! Surely, if anything is clear, it is that Jesus does not want us to toy with the possibility that hell might be bearable. A symbol representing something is never greater than the thing itself.

3. Disintegration

Jesus takes up another figure for hell briefly in Mark 9:48. He is quoting from the Old Testament prophet Isaiah and he speaks about the 'worm that does not die'.

This is a picture which suggests that in hell there is an eternal dissolution which never ceases. Hell is a place of continual disintegration of people and personalities. Perhaps the nearest illustration we can use from our present experience is that of a sleepless night caused by worry. There is something upon your mind that causes you deep anxiety. The prospect of it scares you and drains you of all energy. The worry gets you nowhere and yet you cannot stop worrying about it. You feel as if you are falling apart as a person. You cannot be at peace or feel settled in yourself. It is as if something just keeps gnawing and gnawing away at you, something with which you just cannot come to terms. Jesus, with a love in his heart which does not want us to go there, warns us of the place where the 'worm does not die'. Hell is a place with which no one will ever be able to come to terms.

Hell is for ever

When we are confronted with such desperately solemn descriptions of what hell involves, it can give us no joy to dwell upon them. Such is the awesomeness of this terrible place that, not surprisingly, some people have been drawn to express a hope that the punishments of hell may not be everlasting, but may be terminated by those under God's judgement eventually being annihilated and so no longer suffering. Non-existence and oblivion would certainly be a happy release from hell.

But again, although we sympathize with the compassionate feelings which may draw people to hold out such a hope, it really is not possible to square this with what Jesus teaches. Jesus does not teach annihilation. He teaches a suffering in hell which goes on and on for ever and from which there is no release.

At least three considerations shut us in to the sad truth of the eternity of hell.

1. Heaven and hell are constantly spoken of by Jesus as being the final states of men and women. Jesus does not give us any indication that there is another state beyond hell, namely non-existence achieved through annihilation.
2. Jesus speaks plainly of eternal punishment and eternal fire. He uses the word 'eternal' and he does so quite deliberately. It is sometimes argued that the New Testament word *αιωνιος*, which is translated 'eternal', has more to do with quality of life than duration. But whereas it cannot be denied that there is some reference to quality, its primary meaning does concern duration. Even a cursory glance at a Greek lexicon confirms this. For example the famous Arndt-Gingrich Lexicon records only three meanings of the word *αιωνιος*. It can mean 'without beginning', 'without end' or 'without beginning or end'. Its fundamental meaning concerns duration. The connotation of endless conscious punishment cannot be avoided, much as we may like to avoid it.
3. In Matthew 25:46, at the end of the parable of the sheep and the goats, Jesus tells us, 'Then they will go away to eternal punishment, but the righteous to eternal life.' The same word *αιωνιος*, 'eternal', is used to describe both heaven and hell. If we take the position that hell is capable of termination then, to be consistent, we must believe that the same is true of heaven. But, from the rest of the Bible, that is plainly not the case. Heaven is *for ever*. We must stay with the plain meaning of the word 'eternal'. Both heaven and hell are without end.

The purpose of Jesus' teaching

Now why did Jesus tell us these most profoundly disturbing things? It was because he knew them to be the truth and was desperately anxious to warn people of their need of rescue from being on the road to hell. Men and women spend their lives seeking to accumulate wealth or the comforts of prestige and material possessions. But Jesus taught that nothing in this world is ultimately worth anything unless you are sure that you are not going to that place. It was in the light of hell that Jesus said, 'What good is it for a man to gain the whole world, yet forfeit his soul?' (Mark 8:36.)

Jesus knew how people would react to what he said. He knew that it would not be popular. He knew that many people would ignore his warnings and try to dismiss his teaching from their minds. But he counselled his hearers that hell is real and they should let no obstacle stand in their way and spare no exertion to avoid its terrors. 'Enter through the narrow gate,' said Jesus, 'for wide is the gate and broad is the road that leads to destruction, and many enter through it. But small is the gate and narrow the road that leads to life, and only a few find it' (Matthew 7:13, 14).

The description of hell which emerges from Jesus' teaching is fearful. It is the most horrendous thing we can ever imagine. Knowing the character of Jesus, we cannot for a moment suppose that he merely intended to play upon people's fears in telling us such things. If Jesus was ignorant upon these profound subjects he had no right to set out such a dreadful picture to torment people's imaginations. Still less would he be justified in telling us such things if, being perfectly aware of the true nature of life after death, he knew that there was no such place as hell. It will not do to think that Jesus was using the ends to justify the means – to paint a terrible picture of hell simply in order to scare people into living a moral life, or into believing in him as a Saviour. Jesus was not that kind of man. Jesus was always a man of love and truth. He would not set out such a picture if he had not been completely sure of it and he certainly would not tell lies. Knowing the character of Jesus, we have got to say that he was simply being straight with us.

5.
Is sin that serious?

In the light of what we have seen of Jesus' teaching on hell, we must now return to think about the idea of just punishment.

We ask, 'How can a God of love send sinners to hell?' We ask that question often because it is the extremity of the punishment which appals us. In chapter 3 we considered just punishment, but an eternity in hell seems so unjust. It seems like a punishment which is out of all proportion to the crime. For ever in the pains of hell, and for sins which appear to many of us to be such small things. How can this in any way be right? Where is the justice in it?

One of the greatest problems for people, when they hear what Christians are saying, is that they find it difficult to feel that they are sinners, or that sin is so very serious. 'I've made a few mistakes. Who hasn't? I'm not perfect, but I'm not that bad. I'm no worse than anyone else.' We say those sort of things to ourselves. 'Sin is not that serious.'

To understand the seriousness with which the Bible views sin, we need first to understand something about God.

The majesty of holiness

We live at a time when very little is held sacred. We have grown up as a generation with satire, cynicism and the joys of debunking pomposity. No doubt there were many hypocritical establishment images which needed debunking. But we have been left as a society without heroes or heroines in the classic sense and, in particular, we have been robbed of any understanding of the sacred or the holy.

The noise and bustle of the modern world contributes to this and can dominate our lives so that we have no time for reflection. But if you are the kind of person who perhaps enjoys the countryside and likes to linger on some ancient hill, or in some quiet forest, or on some lonely beach, then there have probably been times, as you have quietly contemplated the scene, when you have been overcome by a sense of your own smallness. You have felt that you are somehow standing in the presence of something far greater than you, of something somehow beyond and above the world. It has been a special moment. You have felt as if you were standing on holy ground, in a holy place. The experience has left you thoughtful, subdued and humbled. You have said, 'How awesome is this place!' and perhaps you have felt quiet in spirit for hours afterwards.

Many people have such experiences. This is how the poet William Wordsworth describes the aftermath of such an experience he had in the Lake District:

> I through meadows homeward went, in grave
> And serious mood; but after I had seen

That spectacle, for many days my brain
Worked with a dim and undetermined sense
Of unknown modes of being; o'er my thoughts
There hung a darkness, call it solitude
Or blank desertion. No familiar shapes
Remained, no pleasant images of trees,
Of sea or sky, no colours of green fields;
But huge and mighty forms, that do not live
Like living men, moved slowly through my mind
By day, and were a trouble to my dreams.

The German liberal theologian Rudolf Otto invented a word to describe this kind of feeling. It is the word 'numinous', the feeling of a holy place. Otto defined the word 'numinous' in terms of 'mystery', 'tremendousness' and 'fascination'. We feel there is a mystery in this place, something beyond our understanding that disturbs and puzzles us. From the Latin word '*tremendum*' we get our word 'tremor'. The 'tremendousness' of it all is something that makes us tremble, not just with ordinary fear, but a trembling which is a response to something beyond and unnervingly different from ourselves. But there is also a fascination. We are afraid and yet we want more; we are drawn to the place, we are enchanted by it.[11] I wonder if you have had an experience like that?

If you have, it will help you to understand something of the overwhelming awesomeness and holiness of God. For what we may have felt of the 'numinous' when we have been humbled and subdued by the tremendousness of creation is what people who meet with God feel, but magnified a thousand times as they stand in the living presence of the terrifyingly majestic Lord of all. Their experience does not just leave them humbled and subdued for an hour or two. It totally reshapes their lives so that they are never the same again, having met with the indescribably awesome, holy God.

Here is the experience of a man called Isaiah, who in the Bible describes what happened to him: 'In the year that King Uzziah died, I saw the Lord seated on a throne, high and exalted, and the train of his robe filled the temple. Above him were seraphs, each with six wings: With two wings they covered their faces, with two they covered their feet, and with two they were flying. And they were calling to one another: "Holy, holy, holy is the Lord Almighty; the whole earth is full of his glory." At the sound of their voices the doorposts and thresholds shook and the temple was filled with smoke. "Woe to me!" I cried. "I am ruined! For I am a man of unclean lips, and I live among a people of unclean lips, and my eyes have seen the King, the Lord Almighty"' (Isaiah 6:1–5).

If we are going to understand something of the seriousness with which the Bible views sin, here is the best place to start. We must try to grasp something of the overwhelming majesty of the living God. It was only as Isaiah was in God's presence that he felt the huge weight of the true seriousness of sin. Because sin is sin against this majestic eternal God, he cries out spontaneously, 'Woe to me!'

The picture of God which Isaiah brings before us reminds us of a great Eastern king, seated upon his throne, with his servants, the angelic seraphs, breathlessly waiting for him to indicate his will and they will be off immediately to obey. But this is no earthly king. Although Isaiah describes many things, the angels, the temple, the seraphic song, yet you will note that no attempt is made in what Isaiah wrote to describe what the one on the throne looks like. All we have is the assertion that Isaiah saw him enthroned and thus exercising his authority. In this refusal to describe him we see the unspeakable majesty of the heavenly King. Isaiah cannot describe him, for it is he whom no mortal man can look upon and live. It is he before whom even sinless heavenly beings like the seraphs feel constrained to cover their faces. It is he before whose face heaven and earth flee away. It is the King of kings.

Isaiah stresses the height of his throne: it is 'high and exalted'. The very hem of his garment completely fills the temple. In telling us such things Isaiah is conveying to us the fact that this King transcends all earthly dimensions. He is truly tremendous in the full meaning of that word. But the great impression which affects both the angelic seraphs and Isaiah himself is the holiness of God: his complete and utter separateness from sin. They recognize with a profundity which reaches to the very depths of their beings that 'God is light; in him there is no darkness at all' (1 John 1:5). He is of purer eyes than even to look upon sin (Habakkuk 1:13). And so the angels are left chanting the holiness of God, while Isaiah is overcome with a sense of his own moral dirtiness and uncleanness. He is in an inward agony as he suddenly realizes what sin is. We never really see what sin is until we have seen God.

As a student, I studied at university near Brighton on the south coast of England. During that time I loved to visit the seashore, not during the summer like most people, but during the winter. There the great majestic waves of the English Channel broke upon the beach, coming down from heights of six or even ten feet. It was a breath-taking sight. But Isaiah had seen something far bigger. He had seen the tidal wave of the holy majesty of the living God. It was only then that he fully realized what sin was. All sin is an arrogant offence and a flagrant insult against this unspeakably glorious person who is our God and our Creator.

An infinite obligation

The Bible teaches the eternal punishment of unrepentant sinners and it does so because sin is an infinite evil. What do we mean? We all realize that some crimes are more odious, or are of greater enormity than others. Consider three different situations in which a person kills another person. There is the case in which an armed burglar breaks into a house and in self-defence, as his life is threatened, the occupier of the house kills the burglar. We look upon that in one way. We look upon the situation in which the mugger kills the defenceless old lady in a totally different way. He was not threatened by her. It is a purely wanton crime. But we view the crime as being even more odious and of even greater enormity if the old lady whom the mugger knowingly murders happens to be the criminal's mother, who has brought him into the world, cared for him and given the best years of her life for his good. Murder is always abhorrent, but for a person to be so selfish and callous as to murder his own loving mother, we would view as an even more heinous crime. We are obligated in a special way to our parents, who have loved and provided for us and anyone who, in a fit of selfishness, can murder a parent, we feel must be especially heartless and evil.

The murder of a mother is a greater evil because it is breaking a great obligation placed on us by love. But sin is an infinite evil because it is the breaking of an infinite obligation. It is an attack upon the glorious holy God, whom we ought to love. God is our Creator, our Sustainer. He is infinitely good. He is the infinite majestic God whom Isaiah saw and who came humbly in Jesus Christ and he has given us every good and wholesome thing that we have ever enjoyed. He is infinitely lovely and therefore there is an infinite obligation to serve him. Then if you and I do not do this – and we do not – we are breaking that infinite obligation and committing an infinite evil. We commit an infinite evil, which in all justice deserves some form of infinite punishment. Thus the Bible teaches the infinite duration of hell.

There is also another reason for the eternal nature of hell. That is that there is no indication that souls sent to hell cease to sin there. It seems rather that people go on in sin, yet reaping no pleasure from it, blaspheming against God, rebellious against him still and therefore their punishment must continue. The seriousness of sin cannot be overstated.

Now I have told you these things, but if you are not a Christian, I do not expect you to understand how serious sin is. The true awfulness and seriousness of sin is something only truly understood and felt when, as with Isaiah, God himself, through his Holy Spirit, begins to deal with a person.

I am suggesting to you that our indifference, our lack of feeling for sin, is not an indicator that sin is not serious, but rather it is a measure simply of how unfeeling we are. It is a measure of how far out of touch with God we are, how far gone we are. It is like a man who is drunk. He feels no pain. He feels nothing. But that is not a measure of good health, or that everything in his life is rosy. It is a measure of how drunk he is, how far out of touch with reality he is; it is a measure of how far gone he is.

Our society shows every sign of being very far gone. For all our self-congratulation that we live in enlightened times, we live in an indifferent and unfeeling culture. In Britain at the present time there are over three million people unemployed. That is something like one in eight of the work force. But often the attitude is that 'as long as it's not me', it does not matter too much. We are indifferent. The south-east of England is unfeeling about the needs of the north. We live in an unfeeling society. Since 1967, two million little babies have been killed in our abortion clinics. All those little lives torn to pieces! But we are indifferent. It was not our life that was terminated. The famine there has been recently in Ethiopia and the Sudan was forecast years before the disaster actually struck. But we in the West were indifferent. It was only when the horror of it was brought slap up against our faces with the TV pictures across our tea tables that we decided to do something. How cold and numb our feelings can be!

Sin brings a blindness, a numbness in ourselves. It brings indifference. It brings a lack of sensitivity to what the true nature of sin is. It is only God's Holy Spirit who can open our eyes. Hell is extreme because sin is extreme.

But let us try to see again what the nature of sin is, because sin often wears a mask to fool us. But there is a place where sin was unmasked. There is that hill outside Jerusalem called Calvary, in Aramaic 'Golgotha', the Place of the Skull. Jesus had done nothing wrong. He was totally innocent. On nine separate occasions in the Gospels his innocence and guiltlessness is affirmed even by his confused enemies. His life had been one of doing good, of being truthful and patient. On that day there were many in the land of Palestine who owed their health to his healing touch. There were many who had been saved from the depths of moral degradation and given new hope and purpose and confidence by him. Yet sinful people like us nailed him to the cross.

But that is not all. That is not enough for sin. As they did so, seeing there a man in the agony of death by crucifixion, many jeered and mocked.

Looking upon this innocent, broken Lord Jesus Christ, the best man the world has ever seen, many laughed at him! Others were prepared to spit at him! There is sin with its mask off! That is sin in its true colours. Sin which disguises itself to us under the cloak of 'being a bit of a sport', or 'a little weakness', did that to Jesus, the Son of God. Hell is extreme, because sin is extreme.

In fact, sin is so serious that it took Jesus being crucified to rescue us. At the cross, amidst all the viciousness against Christ, God was lovingly at work. To understand God we need to understand that at Calvary the extremity of hell is matched by the extremity of God's love.

Christ crucified

Why do Christians make so much of the cross of Jesus? It is because through the cross we see that the extreme pains of hell show us also how extreme is God's love for us.

Hell awaits unrepentant sinners. But the message of the Bible is not bad news. It is good news. The incredible good news is that Jesus died, taking that same extreme punishment upon himself as a substitute for everyone who trusts in him. He loves us that much. That is staggering good news. It is love in the extreme. There is a sense in which, on the cross, Jesus went to hell for us, so that we might never have to go there. Can you imagine such love?

The apostle Paul, explaining to the Christian church in Rome what went on at that first Easter time, put it like this concerning Jesus: 'He was delivered over to death for our sins and was raised to life for our justification' (Romans 4:25). Let us consider what that statement means.

Why did Jesus die?

What happened to Jesus? 'He was delivered over to death for our sins.' The cross was not an accident. He was delivered over to death, not just by the crowds baying for his blood. He was delivered over to death by God. God the Trinity, Father, Son and Holy Spirit, was working out a plan at the cross. We will see more of this in a moment. At the cross Jesus the Son was carrying out the Father's will in the power given to him by the Holy Spirit.

It was 'for our sins' that Jesus died. Sin had blighted our world and our lives and broken our relationship with God. Sin deserves to be punished in hell. But instead, for everyone who trusts him, Jesus took the punishment for sin – all of it. Marvellous!

There is a story about a famous lawgiver who lived a long time ago, called Zaleucus. In his country he decreed that whoever was convicted of adultery should have both his eyes put out. The lustful eyes that had led to sin and the disruption of marriage would be put out. It turned out, however, that his own son was brought before him for that very crime. His son seems to have been well liked and all the citizens pleaded with Zaleucus to pardon his son. At length, the father, loving his son, but seeing the necessity for the law to be upheld impartially, decided to do a very remarkable thing. He put out one of his own eyes, and then one of his son's, so tempering justice with mercy. His son, the wrongdoer, paid half the penalty and he himself paid the other half. That is love, isn't it![12] But Christ's love for us is immeasurably greater. Jesus, you see, did not divide, or share half the penalty for our sin with us. He took it all. Jesus did not just lose an eye for us; he lost his life. Zaleucus did what he did for his son, who loved him, but Jesus did it for us, who when he died had no love at all for him, were indifferent to him or perhaps even hated him. He took the full extreme penalty which we deserved for our sins. He suffered hell for us. He did it as our substitute so that we can be free! 'He was delivered over to death for our sins.'

Jesus could do this because he had no sins of his own to pay for. He was totally innocent.

'But hold on,' says someone, 'isn't it rather immoral of God to punish an innocent person in our place?' Yes, it would be, if it were not for the fact that Jesus was God himself. God the Judge was prepared to have the sentence meted out upon himself, so that justice could be done but we could be saved.

Jesus was God become man. It was this fact, of being the infinite God as well as a man, that enabled Jesus, in the hours he was upon the cross, to bear the infinite punishment which sin deserves. An ordinary man could not have done it, but the Lord Jesus Christ, the God-man, could. He has done it and it is good news for all who trust him.

How can we be sure?

How do we know that Jesus actually accomplished paying for our sins? Lots of people died on crosses in first-century Palestine. How do we know that the death of Jesus was different from all the rest? How can we be sure that sin has been paid for? Paul answers that question in the second part of the verse we have been thinking about. He says that Jesus 'was raised to life for our justification'. The resurrection of Jesus is vitally important.

It should not surprise us that God could raise Jesus from the dead. If he is the God who created the universe, he is capable of doing such things. If he made the universe and all the scientific laws, then obviously God can operate outside them and over and above the laws of nature. He would have had to do this to create those laws in the first place.

But what was the point of God raising Jesus from death? Was it a sort of pointless grand finale, of God displaying his power? No. It had a definite purpose. One thing the resurrection does is that it provides evidence for us that Jesus knew what he was talking about when he spoke about heaven and hell. We should believe what Jesus said about life after death, because he has been through death and come back. He was not just quickly resuscitated after his heart stopped beating for a few moments. He was in the tomb for three days. He went all the way beyond death and returned. Other people can only speculate about what is beyond death. We can only have theories about what is beyond the grave. But Jesus knows. He has been there.

But there is another aspect of the purpose of the resurrection in Paul's mind, as he tells us that Jesus 'was raised to life for our justification'. In a law court when the judge declares someone guilty, he is said to condemn the person. But when the judge declares someone innocent, so that he is released and can walk from the court a free man, the judge is said to 'justify' the man. Raising Jesus from the dead was God's way of declaring that our sin has been completely dealt with by the death of Jesus and we have no more charges to face. It is God's way of showing that we are clear, we are justified.

To put it another way, the purpose of the resurrection can be seen like this. Probably every one of us at some time has walked into an office to pay a bill of some kind – perhaps the rates, or a telephone bill. We handed the money over to the cashier. The cashier counted our money to make sure that we had enough to pay and then he took the bill and gave us a receipt which declared that all was paid. Perhaps as a receipt he gave us back part of the original bill with the words stamped on it, 'Paid in full'. We could then never be asked to pay that bill again. If we were, we could just produce the receipt.

The Lord Jesus Christ walked up to Calvary which was, as it were, God's cash desk for the payment of the bill of our sins. In those six dreadful hours on the cross he was punished for our sins and as he died he paid our debt in full. There was no other way that the account could be settled apart from sinners going to hell. But he did it with his own blood. It is interesting that one of the last things that Jesus said before he died was 'It is finished' (John 19:30). Jesus spoke Aramaic. But in the Greek in which the New Testament records what Jesus said, 'It is finished' is just one word, *tetelestai*. Interestingly, that was the word used in Greek commerce to show that a bill had been paid. It was equivalent to our 'paid in full'. By his death he had paid it completely and God the Father reached out, as a cashier might stamp a bill as 'paid in full', and raised his Son Jesus from the dead as a sign that there was nothing more to pay.

Lots of people died on crosses in first-century Palestine. How do we know that Jesus died for our sins? The answer is because God raised him from the dead.

How do we know that Jesus paid it all, and not just half or some other proportion of our sin? Because the wages of sin is eternal death and if he had only dealt with half our sin he would have had to stay dead. Death could say to him, 'I cannot let you go yet, the bill has not been fully paid.' But he is alive, showing that death had no more hold on him. The resurrection is most important and most assuring.

God invites us to trust Christ. He invites us to faith because Christ has done all this, in the words of Paul, 'for us who believe in him who raised Jesus our Lord from the dead' (Romans 4:24).

So completely has Christ dealt with the sins of his people that the Bible can describe it like this: 'As far as the east is from the west, so far has he removed our sins from us' (Psalm 103:12).

The distance between east and west is immeasurable; they never meet. Christ has so dealt with our sins that Christ's people will never face the penalty of their sins. It has been pointed out that you can start moving north at any place on earth and, if you continued in that direction, you would eventually end up going south. But that is not true when you go east or west. If you start west and continue in that direction, you will always be going west. North and south meet at the poles, but east and west never meet. So far have our sins been removed from us by what Christ has done.

What do you think of Christ?

But perhaps at this point we have another opportunity to see the callous nature and seriousness of sin. We have been to Calvary to see the callousness of human sin, but, non-Christian reader, dare I suggest that there is another place where we can see sin with its mask off. Let me take you to your own heart.

Let me take you there because here is the gospel and God himself has, as it were, gone to hell. The infinite God-man Jesus Christ has suffered the infinite pains of hell, as he bore God's wrath upon the cross, and this has been done in such a way that now he offers you free forgiveness of sins and reconciliation to God through his death. He calls you to himself and asks you to repent of your sins and trust in him. All that was accomplished through his pain and agony at the cross is offered to you and is offered because he loves you and desires to see you rescued. But perhaps still your sinful heart refuses such love and still says 'no'. When Christ has done so much for you, you still say 'no'. There is sin with its mask off! Can you not see that it is the most incredible and indescribable ungratefulness to refuse the overtures of the Lord Jesus Christ, who has done so much for us? Can you not feel the callous indifference that sin has worked in you and with which you concur? Can't you see that sin is an infinite evil? The question perhaps we should be asking is not 'How can a God of love send unrepentant sinners to hell?', but 'How can men and women go on rejecting God who has loved them so much?' There is the tragic marvel! How can they?

Although hell is eternal, not everyone suffers to the same degree in hell. There is always justice in God's dealings with sinners. All sin is serious, but not all sin is equally serious. To sin ignorantly is one thing, but to sin with a full knowledge of what you are doing and the implications of what you are doing is quite another. To sin the first time is wretched, but to repeat the same sin is to increase our guilt. In a very sobering statement the apostle Paul speaks to us of unrepentant sinners increasing the judgement they face, saving up judgement as we might save up money in a bank, waiting for our big pay day when we draw it all out: 'Because of your stubbornness and your unrepentant heart, you are storing up wrath against yourself for the day of God's wrath' (Romans 2:5).

Murder and hatred are serious sins. Adultery

and sexual perversion, such as went on in the Old Testament cities of Sodom and Gomorrah, are serious sins, but we would be wrong to think that these are the most terrible sins of all. It seems the most serious sin a human being can commit is, with the full knowledge of God's love to us in Christ, to despise that love and ignore the claims of Jesus upon our lives. There is a very moving incident in the Gospels where Jesus, no doubt with an aching heart, had to warn those who continually refused his claims despite all his efforts to win them: 'Then Jesus began to denounce the cities in which most of his miracles had been performed, because they did not repent. "Woe to you, Korazin; Woe to you, Bethsaida! If the miracles that were performed in you had been performed in Tyre and Sidon [Gentile cities], they would have repented long ago in sackcloth and ashes. But I tell you, it will be more bearable for Tyre and Sidon on the day of judgement than for you. And you, Capernaum, will you be lifted up to the skies? No, you will go down to the depths. If the miracles that were performed in you had been performed in Sodom, it would have remained to this day. But I tell you that it will be more bearable for Sodom on the day of judgement than for you"' (Matthew 11: 20–24).

Knowing the love of Jesus for us, even for the most hardened and bitter sinners, it is little wonder that at the end of the same chapter in which he denounced the unrepentant cities, who had been so privileged to see his miracles, we find Christ giving one last call for them to turn to him and be saved: 'Come unto me, all you who are weary and burdened, and I will give you rest. Take my yoke upon you and learn from me, for I am gentle and humble in heart, and you will find rest for your souls' (Matthew 11:28, 29).

Sin is serious, but God is serious about saving us.

6.
Isn't God a God of love?

But perhaps, even after all that we have looked at so far, there are still questions in your mind. Even after seeing the amazing love of God to us in Jesus Christ and his cross, you still have some objections and niggling doubts. Maybe you feel that you still cannot face the truth of the Bible's message that we need to fly from the wrath to come and that God has provided the great place of safety and refuge in the Lord Jesus.

Some people would want to say, 'But I still cannot believe that hell is in any way consistent with a God of love.' Let us consider two objections against the gospel of Christ which are often raised at this stage. They may be objections which you have already thought of, or they may not. But they are both worth considering.

1. 'A God of love would never have allowed the human race to fall into sin in the first place.'

The Bible does teach that God is in control. But it does not teach that God is in control in such a way as to leave men and women not responsible for their own actions. It does not teach a theological determinism or fatalism. So it is that the

Lord Jesus, on the night before his death, knowing that he would be betrayed and turned over to his enemies by Judas Iscariot, said to his disciples, 'The Son of Man will go just as it is written about him. But woe to that man who betrays the Son of Man! It would be better for him if he had not been born' (Mark 14:21).

The logic of the objection which says, 'A God of love would never have allowed mankind to fall into sin,' really amounts to an accusation against God. The inference is that he could have stopped it and therefore sin is really his fault. But God made us persons and some measure of self-determination is one of the essential elements distinctive of being human. In this matter of choosing to sin man was a free agent. Sin is not God's fault; it is our choice.

The great nineteenth-century American theologian A. A. Hodge reflects the teaching of the Bible when he writes, 'Free will is a question of great interest. I do not assert, nor is it necessary that I should, what are the essential elements of free agency. Men may differ about that. But we know we have a conscience, and that a person is not a mere machine – for that a machine cannot have an obligation, cannot be subject to command, is certainly proved; but that a person is subject to command, is subject to obligations of conscience, is a matter of universal consciousness. This is very true, more so than any fact of science. . . . How do you prove things? You prove things by deducing the unknown from the known, the uncertain from the certain . . . The things which you start from, which are the means of bringing us results, are more sure than other things which are proved by them. You and I know we are free. You and I know that we are responsible. You and I have that assurance of knowledge which is before all science. This matter of free will underlies everything.'[13]

When God created the first man and woman it was possible for them to sin. But that does not mean that God is responsible for sin. We can misuse any good gift. Let us go back in history to the men who invented the motor car. They nurture the idea, solve the problems, design the machine and set up a car factory. They set out to manufacture cars for the benefit of civilization and as a step forward for their fellow men. They have no intention that the cars should be harmful in any way, but only helpful. But if a car owner decides to get himself drunk and drive at 100 m.p.h. into a brick wall and kill himself, that is not the inventor's fault; he never intended that drivers should do that. He is not responsible; the driver is. We do not arrest the management of the Ford Motor Company or of British Leyland every time there is a drunken driving accident. It would be preposterous. It is equally preposterous and unjust to accuse God of being responsible for our sin.

2. 'Well even if we are guilty, and we do deserve hell, a God of love would step in and do something, even in reckless abandon. A God of love would do anything to save us.'

In answer to this, I have to say that he will not do *anything* to save us. He loves us immensely.

But he will not do anything to save us, because there is something which he rightly loves even more than he loves us. He loves righteousness. King David, writing in the book of Psalms, puts it like this: 'On the wicked he will rain fiery coals and burning sulphur; a scorching wind will be their lot. For the Lord is righteous, he loves justice; upright men will see his face' (Psalm 11:6, 7).

God loves what is right. He will do everything possible to save us, consistent with justice. That is what he has done in Christ. But he will not do anything inconsistent with justice, because there is something even more terrible than sinners going to hell and that is a God who is no longer committed to justice.

'Why doesn't God just let us all off?' Because we are responsible for our sins and God is committed to what is right. To say that God should not punish sin is to ask him to say that sin does not matter. It is to ask him to say that holiness does not matter. It is to ask him to be no longer committed to justice. It is to ask him to be no longer committed to right instead of wrong. Logically it is, to all intents and purposes, to ask him to become an evil God and that he will not do. It is to ask him to accommodate himself to our sin, not by dealing with it justly by hell or by the cross, but by himself becoming like Satan, not committed to what is right. He will not do that. The punishment of sinners is terrible, but far more terrible is the prospect of an omnipotent evil God.

No, God is committed to justice and what is

right. Therefore, if people carry on in their sins and will not repent, he must judge them. He does so with the greatest reluctance. He is slow to anger. He does not delight in the death of a sinner. He is a God of love who calls people to turn to him. But if they will not, he must judge them, to show his total abhorrence of, and opposition to, sin and evil.

'A God of love would do anything to save us!' But you know, he has done everything apart from throwing aside his justice, in order to save you. The utter reckless love of God is displayed at the cross of Jesus. He has a passionate love for sinners: 'God so loved the world that he gave his one and only Son, that whoever believes in him shall not perish but have eternal life' (John 3:16). The New Testament tells us that God delays the promised Day of Judgement: 'The Lord is not slow in keeping his promise, as some understand slowness. He is patient with you, not wanting anyone to perish, but everyone to come to repentance' (2 Peter 3:9).

God's love to us in Christ shows an utter abandon of love. His love to us in Jesus would be absurd were it not so profound. Think of what God has done. God the Son, Jesus Christ, has come and an absurd exchange has taken place in the marvellous abandon of his love. He has taken upon himself our sin and carried it to the cross and borne all the wrath our sins deserve. In exchange for our sins, Jesus has lived a perfectly righteous life in the sight of God and has given that to us in the record books of heaven, that we might be counted right with God. In exchange for our sins, Jesus has given us an open door to eternal life and heaven. In exchange for our sins, Jesus has given us the right to become children of God and for God the Holy Spirit to come and dwell in our hearts. Jesus has said, 'I'll go to hell for you and I'll give you the greatest eternal treasure that anyone can ever imagine!' Here is the overwhelming, unspeakable love of God for mankind.

'Why doesn't God just let us all off?' The answer is that he will, for everyone who turns to him. We must repent of our sins, which are dragging us to hell, and trust in Jesus Christ. For all who will do that, through Jesus and his cross, God lets us off. Here is the love of God.

Jesus weeps for you

On two separate occasions in the Gospel of Luke we find the writer recording Jesus weeping over the city of Jerusalem and its people who had rejected him. Foreseeing the terrible consequences for people who reject him who is God's way of salvation, Jesus weeps: 'O Jerusalem, Jerusalem, you who kill the prophets and stone those sent to you, how often I have longed to gather your children together, as a hen gathers her chicks under her wings, but you were not willing!' (Luke 13:34.) Of the events of Palm Sunday, the Sunday before the Friday on which he died, we read, 'As he approached Jerusalem and saw the city, he wept over it and said, "If you, even you, had only known on this day what would bring you peace – but now it is hidden from your eyes"' (Luke 19:41).

These tears of Jesus assure us of at least four things.

Firstly, they show us that we are very wrong if we suppose that Christ cares for no one but Christians. He came to Jerusalem on the Sunday before his death and his disciples were rejoicing, in carnival mood, as they saw in Jesus God's true King. But it was not for his disciples at this time that Jesus showed his love and concern. He wept over the hard-hearted people of Jerusalem. He knew very well what was going to happen to him there in the next few days – his unjust trial, the false accusations, the crowds roaring for his death, his brutal crucifixion. Yet, knowing all this, Jesus loved and pitied these people. We are very wrong if we think that God loves no one but Christians. Christ cares for all. His compassion extends to every man, woman and child on earth. He cares for you, personally. He has a true love and concern for the person who is rejecting him and is still living for self. He has a love for the one who is still bent on sin. He has a love for the one who is totally indifferent towards him. He has a love for all, as well as the special affection he has for his own people.

Secondly, as Jesus weeps over lost souls, his tears signify the sincerity and tenderness of his love towards you and me. These are not deceitful tears. Remember that Jesus, who shed these tears for you, was prepared to shed his own blood. Jesus did not shed these tears in an artificial pretence, as some kind of show to impress us. He shed them because he truly loves us. We should not refuse the offers of Jesus to us. Consider what love and tender compassion you would be sinning against. These are tears of sincere love to you.

Thirdly, these tears show you that if you persist in rejecting Christ's love and you persist in your impenitency, then there is no hope for you. You are then without remedy. You are lost for ever. Jesus weeps because he foresees the future for those who reject him and are indifferent to him, just as Jerusalem was. He foresees people in hell and weeps for them. Do not think, 'I can reject Jesus, but I may yet be all right, by some other way.' If there was some other way for you, Jesus would not have wept. Instead he would have consoled himself with the thought that 'They might yet escape from the judgement.' But he knew that there is no other way to be saved other than by coming to him, and so he weeps. Jesus foresaw the awful reality of the coming Day of Judgement. 'Then I saw a great white throne and him who was seated on it. Earth and sky fled from his presence, and there was no place for them. And I saw the dead, great and small, standing before the throne, and books were opened. Another book was opened, which is the book of life. The dead were judged according to what they had done as recorded in the books. The sea gave up the dead that were in it, and death and Hades gave up the dead that were in them, and each person was judged according to what he had done. Then death and Hades were thrown into the lake of fire. The lake of fire is the second death. If anyone's name was not found written in the book of life, he was thrown into the lake of fire' (Revelation 20:11–15). As Jesus contemplates the vast scene of eternal judgement, he weeps for those whose names are not written in the book of life of faith in him.

Fourthly, these tears of Jesus signify to us how very eager he is to save people and how gladly he would save you, if you will accept mercy while it may be had. Because, if he weeps over those who are not saved, from the same love he will joyfully receive all who turn to him sincerely. These tears of the Lord Jesus Christ hold out a great promise to us all. These tears signify that Jesus is more than willing to receive you. In all your sins, in all your individuality, perhaps amid all those fears which inwardly tell you that although Christianity might work for others it could never work for you – even amidst all these things, Jesus can and will rescue you. The tears of Jesus show you his love and call you to receive God's mercy and forgiveness in Christ, by personally committing your life to him.

Forgiveness

In our hard-bitten society it can be sometimes quite difficult to believe that there is such a thing as forgiveness. We have come not to really expect it. Whether or not it is actually true I do not know, but it is said that a famous footballer used to keep a black book of the names of those players who had fouled him during a game. When the right opportunity came, he intended to take revenge, to get them back. At work, at school, even in the family we often find things are like that. Even when people say they have forgiven us, we later find that they actually have not. Things from the past are dragged up yet again to put us in our place or get at us. We expect revenge rather than someone ceasing from resentment. We expect a grudge to be nursed rather than forgiveness.

Perhaps it is for that reason that some people find it difficult to realize that God forgives. In the Bible, however, there are many, many promises of God's willingness to forgive us. Let us list a few of them. The prophet Isaiah records God as saying, 'I, even I, am he who blots out your transgressions for my own sake, and remembers your sins no more' (Isaiah 43:25). Again Isaiah has God saying, 'I have swept away your offences like a cloud, your sins like the morning mist. Return to me, for I have redeemed you' (Isaiah 44:22). Another great Old Testament prophet Jeremiah records God saying, 'I will cleanse them from all the sin they have committed against me and will forgive all their sins of rebellion against me' (Jeremiah 33:8). The prophet Micah has a lovely way of speaking of God's forgiveness. In prayer to God he says, 'Who is a God like you, who pardons sins and forgives transgression? . . . You will again have compassion on us; you will tread our sins underfoot and hurl all our iniquities into the depths of the sea' (Micah 7:18,19). So when we come into the New Testament, we find the risen Lord Jesus Christ telling his disciples just before he returned to heaven, 'This is what is written: The Christ will suffer and rise from the dead on the third day, and repentance and forgiveness of sins will be preached in his name to all nations' (Luke 24:46, 47). The apostle John assures us, in one of the letters he wrote to the churches of his day, 'If we claim to be without sin, we deceive ourselves and the truth is not in us. If we confess our sins, he is faithful and just and will forgive us our sins and purify us from all unrighteousness' (1 John 1:8, 9). Our sins deserve hell, but the marvellous and exhilarating news is that, through what Jesus has accomplished for us, we can be forgiven. That forgiveness is free and total. To know that forgiveness is one of the most liberating things that can ever happen to anyone.

Such forgiveness can be a literally life-transforming experience. Many people carry burdens of guilt and fear which cripple them as personalities. It makes them afraid to die and yet scars and damages their lives. But when someone comes to know the free forgiveness of God in Christ there is such release. People can face themselves and they can stand free and erect in the presence of God.

A young friend, Trevor, who was taken along to church and found Christ, put his experience like this: 'When I got there, I found it was not at all what I expected. The place was not plush or ornate, but I remember sensing an air of excitement and people seemed genuinely happy. Amazingly, I actually listened to what was said and it began to make sense. Suddenly, I could clearly see the way my life was going. I was the sinner the preacher was talking about; I needed to get right with God. Inwardly, I began to break down and ended up praying with my head down through most of the second half of the sermon. As I was praying, I can only say that the Lord Jesus himself actually came to me. I was convinced in my head of what had been said and the result was a great experience and sense of peace flooding my heart. I was loved by God! I was forgiven! I had never known anything like this.'

Such pardon and forgiveness has been known by people all down the centuries as they have found Christ. This is how the great eighteenth-century evangelist John Wesley described his own conversion, as he listened to an explanation of the gospel at a meeting in London. 'I felt,' he wrote, 'my heart strangely warmed. I felt I did trust in Christ, Christ alone for salvation; and an assurance was given me that he had taken away *my* sins, even *mine*, and saved *me* from the law of sin and death.'[14]

We need our sins forgiven and forgiveness is available for us in Jesus Christ. God offers you and me a total and free pardon.

How can I find forgiveness?

Imagine a man being rescued from the raging waters of a storm at sea. A lifeline is thrown to him. He grabs that line and holds on to it with both hands. One hand might slip; he does not play around; he grips it with both hands. Similarly, if we are to be saved, we must take hold of Christ with both hands and those hands are called *repentance* and *faith*. The way back to God and his forgiveness involves both turning to him and trusting him, repentance and faith.

Repentance

To illustrate what repentance is, Jesus told one of his most famous parables: 'There was a man who had two sons. The younger one said to his father, "Father, give me my share of the estate." So he divided his property between them. Not long after that, the younger son got together all he had, set off for a distant country and there squandered his wealth in wild living. After he had spent everything, there was a severe famine in that whole country, and he began to be in need. So he went and hired himself out to a citizen of that country, who sent him to his fields to feed pigs. He longed to fill his stomach with the pods that the pigs were eating, but no one gave him anything. When he came to his senses, he said, "How many of my father's hired men have food to spare, and here I am starving to death! I will set out and go back to my father and say to him: Father I have sinned against heaven and against you. I am no longer worthy to be called your son; make me like one of your hired men.' So he got up and went to his father. But while he was still a long way off, his father saw him and was filled with compassion for him; he ran to his son, threw his arms around him and kissed him. The son said to him, "Father I have sinned against heaven and against you.

I am no longer worthy to be called your son." But the father said to his servants, "Quick! Bring the best robe and put it on him. Put a ring on his finger and sandals on his feet. Bring the fatted calf and kill it. Let's have a feast and celebrate. For this son of mine was dead and is alive again; he was lost and is found." So they began to celebrate' (Luke 15:11–24).

The family Jesus describes was in a very bad way. They may have been living together, but, like so many families today, relationships were tense and broken. The younger son despised his dad and could not wait to get away from him. Asking for his share of the inheritance was, in the culture of first-century Palestine, equivalent to saying, 'I want the will read now!' In other words, 'Father, I wish you were dead!' That is such an apt picture of the breakdown of relationships between God and man. We have gone off on our own, not wanting God.

Repentance is what happened in the life of the young son. He repented of what he had done. He changed his mind. This prodigal son recognized that he had sinned. When he came to his senses he faced himself with the fact that the way he was going was useless and wrong and he decided to return home: 'I will set out and go back to my father.' We need to make such a decision to return to God.

He confessed his sin. He was desperately sorry for what he had done. It had done him no good and had been a terrible open insult to his father. He did not try to shift the blame elsewhere for what he had done. He realized that what he had done made him no longer worthy to be called his father's son, such was the affrontery he had perpetrated. Humbly and sorrowfully he was prepared to own up: 'Father, I have sinned against heaven and against you, I am no longer worthy to be called your son.' This was no cheap pretence. It was deep and genuine. In seeking God's forgiveness, we need to get alone and sincerely confess our sins and express genuine regret to God in prayer.

He was now happy and willing to be his father's servant. Before, the last thing in the world he wanted was to live and do what his father told him. He wanted to be free of all restraint. He wanted to live for himself. He wanted to do what *he* wanted to do. But now, since he had seen where that led, his whole attitude had changed. He wanted to serve his father. Perhaps in this way he thought he could begin to make a repair of the terrible insult. Repentance involves us turning from living for self and seeking to truly live for God. Disobedience must be replaced by a willingness for obedience which shows itself in practice. Jesus said, 'If anyone loves me, he will obey my teaching' (John 14:23).

With sorrow for the past in his heart, the son had changed from a stubborn rebel into a humble servant. That is repentance. And that is how we begin to take hold of God's salvation in Christ.

Faith

To illustrate what faith is, we can look at a rather moving incident in the life of Jesus. It was a day when great crowds of people were following

Jesus along the dusty hot roads of Palestine. He was going to a man's house who had asked him to help his sick daughter and he was being jostled and pushed by the people. 'A woman was there who had been subject to bleeding for twelve years. She had suffered a great deal under the care of many doctors and had spent all she had, yet instead of getting better she grew worse. When she heard about Jesus, she came up behind him in the crowd and touched his cloak, because she thought, "If I just touch his clothes, I will be healed." Immediately her bleeding stopped and she felt in her body that she was freed from her suffering. At once Jesus realized that power had gone out from him. He turned round in the crowd and asked, "Who touched my clothes?" "You see the people crowding against you," his disciples answered, "and yet you can ask, 'Who touched me?' " But Jesus kept looking around to see who had done it. Then the woman, knowing what had happened to her, came and fell at his feet and, trembling with fear, told him the whole truth. He said to her, 'Daughter, your faith has healed you. Go in peace and be freed from your suffering' (Mark 5:25–34).

Many people touched and bumped against Jesus that day, but it was only the woman with faith who was healed. She looked to Jesus and believed that what he had done for others he would do for her. She reached out to him expectantly and trustingly. We must come to Jesus in faith, trusting him to rescue us and give us forgiveness. Faith is vital.

Faith is not in itself what puts us right with

God. It is Jesus and his death and resurrection for our sins. But it is only by faith that what Jesus has done is personally applied to us. Faith is like the electric lead to a stereo system. It carries the current. It is not the lead which makes the stereo function, it is the electricity. But until the lead is there and plugged into the supply there is nothing, no music. All that is needed for our forgiveness and to bring God into our lives is in Jesus. But we must take that step of faith. We must trust him. We must commit ourselves to him personally, otherwise all that Jesus has done is of no effect for us. Our sins are still there. Hell still awaits us. But all that is removed and we find complete forgiveness as we turn to God in repentance and put our trust, our faith, in the Lord Jesus Christ.

As we do this, we will find forgiveness and the kind of reception from God which the prodigal son received when he returned. God gives us his love and his Holy Spirit to come and dwell in our hearts to communicate God's strength and love to us. We should repent and believe on Jesus Christ.

God's love and our response

Jesus said, 'Whoever comes to me I will never drive away' (John 6:37). God loves you and is seeking your rescue. Jesus put it like this, 'Suppose a woman has ten silver coins and loses one. Does she not light a lamp, sweep the house and search carefully until she finds it? And when she finds it, she calls her friends and neighbours together and says, "Rejoice with me; I have found my lost coin." In the same way, I tell you, there is rejoicing in the presence of the angels of God over one sinner who repents' (Luke 15:8–10).

God sees you as lost and on your way to hell. But when a sinner turns and trusts Christ and repents, he or she has been found by God and rescued for ever. When this happens, such is God's love that Jesus describes the rejoicing in heaven. God himself, as it were, laughs with joy and breaks into song with delight.

Soberly and reverently you should get alone with God and in prayer commit your life to him, thanking him for all that he has done for us in his glorious Son, Jesus Christ.

Do not let the love of your sins hold you back. This life is soon over and then the fleeting pleasures of sin will be gone for ever. Sin now and hell later is the very worst of bargains. There is forgiveness in Christ.

Do not let what other people will say if you become a Christian stand in your way. Do not let other people send you to hell. Sometimes we need to listen to our friends, but in this matter we need to listen to Jesus.

Take these matters with the greatest seriousness. There is a heaven and a hell. At the beginning of the book it was noted that Jesus had more than anyone else to say on these eternal issues. Jesus would not merely play upon our fears. He is not that kind of character. He would not have spoken as he did unless he was absolutely sure of what he was saying. In his love for us he warns us. In his love for us he went to the cross. In his love he calls us to trust ourselves to him.

Notes

1. Eryl Davies, *The Wrath of God,* Evangelical Press of Wales, 1984, p. 11.
2. J. Bronowski and Bruce Mazlish, *The Western Intellectual Tradition*, Penguin Books, 1963, p. 52.
3. Quoted in *Lion Handbook of Christian Belief,* Lion Publishing, p. 343.
4. C. S. Lewis, *On Punishment*, Marcham Books, p. 3.
5. Norman Tutt, 'Justice or Welfare?', *Social Work Today,* vol. 14, no 7, 1982, p. 8.
6. Garth Wood, *The Myth of Neurosis*, Macmillan 1983, pp. 47, 48.
7. C. E. M. Joad, Quoted in *The Case for Christianity* by Colin Chapman, Lion Publishing, p. 71.
8. C. S. Lewis, *op cit*, p. 5.
9. Norman Tutt, *op cit*, pp. 9, 6.
10. H. M. Carson, *The Biblical Doctrine of Eternal Punishment*, Carey Conference Paper, 1978, p. 14.
11. Robin Pearce, *Faith and Experience*, Henry Walter, 1975, p. 12.

12. John Flavell, *Works,* vol. 1, Banner of Truth, p. 185.
13. A. A. Hodge, *Evangelical Theology*, Banner of Truth, pp. 156, 157.
14. Arnold Dallimore, *George Whitefield*, vol. 1, Banner of Truth, p. 186.